Father George giv

three minutes of love, kindness, generosity and spirituality. I think Sir Winston Churchill said something that really makes Father's talks—puts what Father does so well—into perspective: ". . . sure I can give a speech to Parliament. A thirty-minute speech will take me three hours to prepare; a three-minute speech will take me three days . . ." All that and he never fails to make me feel better about me, you and God.

—Captain Jack Huffman,
Southwest Airlines Pilot

Father George's homilies and his airport bulletins are not just items for myself, my boyfriend and his friends. We share his words and pass those words back and forth. We marvel at their inspirational simplicity.

—Beth Roberts,
Southwest Airlines Flight Attendant

Father McKenna's homilies contain sound, practical, spiritual advice. They take only three minutes to listen to, but leave me pondering their message for a long time. His homilies touch the heart and nourish the soul.

—Judge Thomas Mescall,
Probate Judge, Albuquerque, NM

Father McKenna's homilies are spiritual gems from a seasoned veteran of life. He has 'been there, done that.' His talks are time-tested wisdom expressed in metaphor and simile by one of Chicago's great story tellers.

—Tom Cusack, Insurance Agent, Oak Lawn, IL

At a time in my life when everything felt out of control and the stress was killing me, Father McKenna's homilies inspired me to change my life 180 degrees. I felt like Father was speaking just to me. His words of wisdom gave me the hope and courage I needed to do what was best for my family.

—Judith Gilbert, Marketing Professor,
Roosevelt University, Chicago, IL

I would like to thank Father McKenna for providing Midway Airport employees and the traveling public a forum for worship at the airport. We greatly appreciate his many contributions over the years and look forward to his continued spiritual guidance in the future.

—Erin O'Donnell
Deputy Commissioner,
Chicago Midway Airport

In the early part of 1989, I was introduced to the airport chapel. It must have been fate because at the time I was missing something in my spirituality and the timing was perfect. Once I started going to Mass, I realized what a spiritual man Father McKenna was. He had a gentleness about him that put you at ease. He is called a holy man by his peers.

When he gives a sermon, it always includes some experience of his and usually adds some of his great sense of humor. His sermons only last three to three and a half minutes and in that short time he says more than most people say in thirty minutes.

I must say my nine years of knowing Father McKenna has a special meaning in my heart. I consider it a privilege to know him and I thank God that He made it possible.

—Matt Marich, Dept. of Aviation,
Chicago Midway Airport

"I'll only speak for 3 minutes." Don't you wish every priest would say that! Seriously though, after years of listening to long-winded preachers, Father McKenna's three-minute, spiritually power-packed homilies are a breath of fresh air.

—James E. Higgins III
Publisher, Astrologer, Former Seminarian

I'LL ONLY SPEAK FOR 3 MINUTES

VOLUME 1

I'll Only Speak for 3 Minutes

VOLUME 1

Spiritual Inspirations That Will Change Your Life!

Father George McKenna

Vedic Cultural Association Publishing
Honolulu • Los Angeles • Chicago

I'll Only Speak for 3 Minutes
Vedic Cultural Association Publishing / August 1998

Book design by Symes Production & Design
Design concept by Joseph P. Higgins

Cover Photo by Carrie Leubben
Expressly Portraits
Chicago Ridge, IL
Debra Bragg, Manager

Printed in the United States of America

ISBN 0-89213-248-5

To
Padre Pio
who answered our prayers
and made possible
the Chicago Midway Airport Chapel.

Printed with Permission
National Centre for Padre Pio, Inc.
2213 Old Route 100
Barto, PA 19504

Contents

Introduction

I first met Father McKenna while attending Quigley Preparatory Seminary South. All the seminarians loved Father for his kindness, humility and wisdom. Twenty-five years and many, many travels later, I began visiting Chicago frequently while working on a book about my life as an astrologer to multi-billionaire Doris Duke. I would often attend Mass at the airport chapel with my mother. There I met Father McKenna once again.

One day, as Father started his homily with the words, "I will only speak for three minutes," I had a flash of divine inspiration. "That's a book," I exclaimed to myself. I mentioned this to my mother, brother and sister. They all loved the idea. We then approached Father, who enthusiastically embraced the concept. In fact, he had always wanted to publish, but had no idea how to go about it. I assured him that we could do it.

What follows is the amazing story of how Father started the chapel at Midway Airport and 37 of his famous three-minute homilies.

—James E. Higgins III

The Inside Story of Midway Chapel

One cold January day, while sitting in the terminal of Midway Airport, I said to myself, "Wouldn't it be a good thing if religious services could be held somewhere here. It is now January, 1987, and not one religious service has been held at the airport since its opening in 1927."

I put this possibility before Padre Pio, whom I had admired from the early days of my priesthood. As a Capuchin monk in Italy, he had inspired so many people with his strong faith in the Mass and the Eucharist. In the history of the Catholic Church, Padre Pio has been the only priest bearing the stigmata of all five wounds of Christ.

A year before the Midway Chapel was to open, I found myself at a house for priests in Paris, the Foyer Sacerdotal. Come dinner time, we had the choice of forty different places in the dining room. Strangely, one French priest came and sat next to me for the three evenings he spent there.

An American priest, on the third night, asked this French priest for me what kind of work he did. His answer stunned me, "I am Father Andre. I am in charge of promoting the cause of Padre Pio for Sainthood in all of France."

Father Andre went on to tell me, through our American interpreter, that he had known Padre Pio well and had gone regularly for confession to this holy man. From his station wagon, this priest gave me many photos of the stigmatic priest, who had died in 1948. I promised Padre Pio that we would always have his photo in our airport chapel if he brought about its opening. We have kept our promise.

In the year 1987 and the first months of 1988, the people of Our Lady of the Snows Parish, located a few blocks from the airport, prayed for the opening of the Midway Chapel. As an associate pastor in the parish, I had shared my dream with them.

At this same time, I visited a parish friend dying of cancer: Bill Sikon. As we sat together, he wrote on a piece of paper, "Chapel—how does it look?"

I said to Bill, "When you get to Heaven in a few days, you will have to pray for us." He died within the week.

A few days later a big breakthrough took place, where before there had not been hope for it. Was Bill working for us in Heaven? His interest in the chapel amazed me. With death at his elbow, Bill was asking about its future.

Mr. Bill Krystiniak, then Alderman of our airport ward, stepped forward to become a key person in dealing with the Department of Aviation of the City of Chicago. Without him, we would have made little progress in convincing others of the worthiness of a chapel in the airport.

I believe Padre Pio inspired both these Bills to become such devoted friends of the chapel.

Even when Cardinal Bernadin and the city officials gave their permission for religious services to be held in Midway Airport, no one could find a place for the chapel. Was our dream of a place of worship in Midway Airport to stop at this point, after eighteen months of effort and prayer? People in Our Lady of the Snows were offering their pains and sicknesses to God for its opening. We thank all these unknown saints for their unselfish help.

Suddenly, Midway Airlines, under the direction of Mr. David Hinson, came up with a most generous offer. Midway Airlines, to its great credit, gave us the use of one of its gates on Saturday evenings and Sunday mornings. All Midway Airlines employees, and indeed all the airport workers and people of other airlines, have shown the chapel workers a courtesy and a spirit of helpfulness far beyond the call of duty.

We have prayed for the success of the airlines and the good health of their employees and all other airport workers at every Mass offered during these last ten years at Midway.

At the first Mass ever celebrated in Midway Airport—Saturday, July 24, 1988—a young woman guitarist, Miss Erin Solkowski from Our Lady of the Snows Parish, accompanied the overflowing congregation in song. This was her only visit to the airport chapel. No one else has ever played a musical instrument in the celebration of our Masses.

A few weeks later, Erin's mother told me an amazing story. Erin's middle name is Pio, given at birth. Ann Solkowski needed help at the birth of Erin and prayed to Padre Pio, promising that she would name the child—boy or girl—Pio. Erin was delivered safely. Padre Pio was saying at that first Mass in the airport, "See, I am with you." Thank you, Padre Pio.

—Father George McKenna

Midway Airport Acknowledgments

In addition to Padre Pio, Bill Sikon, Bill Krystiniak, the late Joseph Cardinal Bernadin and David Hinson, I would also like to thank and acknowledge others who were instrumental in starting Midway Airport Chapel: Congressman William Lipinski; former Midway Airport Manager, Richard DiPietro; Mayor Richard M. Daley; Richard Gudzior; Gene Zell of Zell Printing; Joe Waddell RIP; Reverend Daniel Holihan; and the Midway Chapel Volunteer Workers.

Book Acknowledgments

This book would never have seen the light of day without the help of these good friends mentioned here. Initially, they proposed the idea of the book's publication and then carried through in every aspect of making it a reality: James E. Higgins III (publisher), Joseph Higgins (designer) and Judith Higgins Gilbert (marketing). My sincere thanks to them for their encouragement and cooperation.

The Resurrection Of My Spirit

Some time ago, a vast area of Texas had received no rainfall for seven years. The countryside took on the appearance of a moonscape—no vegetation, the topsoil three inches deep in dust, signs of death everywhere. One day, the real estate people, on an inspection trip, agreed that the land should go for a dollar an acre. "Nothing will ever grow here again," they said.

Then the rains came in torrential downpours for eight days, bringing about a miracle of Nature. Overnight, tiny flowers with blue blossoms, called sunbonnets, carpeted the prairies with a breathtaking beauty. Shortly afterwards, crops of oats came up on farms where no one had sown oats for years. Even more amazing, good fields of wheat grew after the oats—something hard to believe, because no one had planted seeds for wheat for an even longer time.

This story encourages me to look at the "landscape" of my inner spirit. Perhaps I am selling myself short on the possible qualities of goodness that might lie hidden there. A reader might be thinking: "I have ill will towards many people, something that will stay with me until death. Despite all my efforts, I have never had this quality of love in my spirit. My soul looks like a shambles, with little beauty in it. These years thinking only of myself have drained all life out of it. My destiny is set without any more changes to be made."

"Nonsense!" says Jesus, the Lord of the Resurrection, "you are not a hopeless case. Start thinking of the kind of person you wish to be. Mention these qualities to Me in prayer at this Eastertime while having complete trust in My power to bring these virtues into your life. I am the Lord of Life."

In past years, at Eastertime, I have thrilled at the changes the Risen Lord brought about in the lives of His friends. How unhappy, discouraged and frightened the disciples were at the death of the Master, ready to return to catching fish for their livelihood. Once the Lord appeared and talked with them, their mood of despondency disappeared. Why cannot Christ do this for all of us, His followers in the 20th century?

"Nonsense!" says Jesus, the Lord of the Resurrection, "you are not a hopeless case."

I am going to spell out clearly for the Lord of Eastertime the kind of person I desire to be. Why should anyone be burdened with a short temper, with a careless tongue that slashes away at the self-esteem of others? There is a better way to live, to bring peace to a violent world. The Lord of the Resurrection will enter my desolate soul at my request and bring forth crops of goodness and beauty.

Tell others about the opening story above, especially those with sad faces and unlaughing eyes!

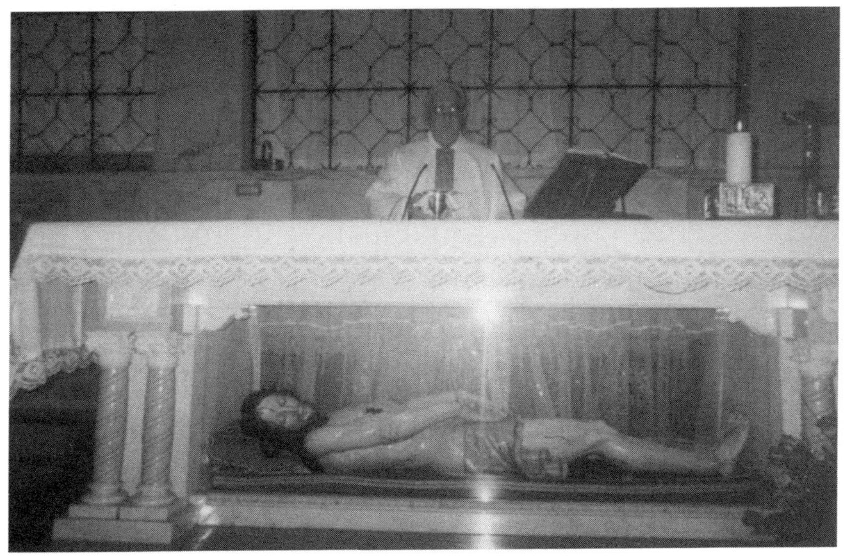

Tomb of Padre Pio in Foggia, Italy.

The Victory Of The Cross

Here follows a true story—one that has affected my life greatly through the years, although I have not written or preached much about it.

In the Vietnam War, a U.S. Marine fighter pilot found himself a prisoner of war in a miserable cell after being shot down by a ground-to-air missile. As he threw himself down on the frozen dirt floor, darkness and despair filled his heart. As a God-fearing man, he knew he couldn't survive the cold, the heat, the poor food, the frequent torture sessions without God's help.

What could he do to bring God's presence into his cell in some visible way? What would the reader do in this situation? After some thought, the pilot took off his military shoe and, with the leather heel, scraped a cross on the cement wall. Through the months and years ahead, he made this his place of prayer, with his thoughts usually centered on the Cross of Christ.

"Christ came to show me how to live," this man of faith kept saying to himself. "In the Garden of Gethsemane, the Lord accepted His cup of suffering from the Father when He said, 'Not my will but Thine be done.' "

So, the American pilot, each day, accepted the hardships of prison life and offered his pain-filled hours to the Father in union with the Passion of Christ on the Cross. A few years later, he left the prison, strong in spirit and deeply in love with life.

We all carry crosses of suffering! One writer wrote that no adult human being has perfect health. This leaves the door open to much pain, discomfort and stresses of all kinds. What about the struggle to pay bills, to live with heartbreaks, and the challenging temptations swirling about us all day long!

What could he do to bring God's presence into his cell in some visible way?

Suffering has no value in itself. Only when we unite our hardships to the sufferings of Christ on the Cross do we profit from life's misfortunes. At this Resurrection time, we witness the Triumph of the Cross of Christ. From the darkness of the Hill of Calvary, the Lord went to the brightness of Easter morning. Likewise, for us, we will experience a glorious resurrection of spirit, not only for everlasting life, but, even now, in this earthly life.

"Father, I accept my cross of discomfort out of love for You! Take my offering as You did for Your Son and continue to help me to carry my cross with courage and faith." We thank our nameless Marine pilot for sharing the drama of his prison life with us.

I feel a tremendous uplift of spirit when, in the despair of physical and mental pain, I use the words above. My cross becomes a bridge by which I pass from the land of darkness to the land of light.

The Beauty Of A Personal Resurrection

Jerusalem, Wednesday, January 4th, 1995. This morning, my four friends—all laymen—and I come to the Church of the Holy Sepulcher to offer Mass in the Tomb of Christ. At 4:45 am, as dawn breaks, we walk to the Church from our residence at the First Station, along the Via Dolorosa (the Way of the Cross), a distance of three blocks. We move along in silence, thinking such deep thoughts about the Man Who had dragged Himself along this same Way.

Entrance to the Garden of Gethsemani.

Five people can fit comfortably in the inner alcove of the Tomb where the Mass of Easter is said every day, except in Holy Week. This morning, our group of five and two others have crowded into this place of heaven-like peace.

One of these others is Sister Paracleta, who stands just back of my right shoulder, an Ethiopian nun whose name means the Holy Spirit. Never have I met another Sister Paracleta in the world. The unexpected presence of this holy person, a hermit near the Garden of Gethsemane, assures me that the Holy Spirit has come to inspire me and my companions in our search for a deeper friendship with Christ.

The unexpected presence of this holy person, a hermit near the Garden of Gethsemane, assures me …

With only candles to light up our low-ceiling chapel, we proceed with the joyous words of the Easter story, replete with Alleluias: "Praise the Lord. This is the day the Lord has made. Let us rejoice and be glad." Although I have offered Mass here many times in past years, this morning I feel lifted out of my body with a peace and joy beyond all understanding. Those with me in the Tomb are experiencing the same feelings they later tell me at breakfast: The Lord is risen, Alleluia. He has kept His word and promises. We can believe all the other wonderful things He has told us.

At our tasty breakfast, the jubilant voices and shining eyes of my fellow pilgrims tell me that Christ has the secret to all happiness. These men with me have followed vocations in the world, but no accomplishments in their work have ever brought so much delight and satisfaction to their hearts as has our Mass of the Resurrection in the Tomb of Christ this morning.

In our later sharings of thoughts, these good-hearted men tell how overcome they are to feel the rewards of friendship with the Risen Christ. Months afterwards, they spell out with enthusiasm how the Mass in the Tomb still fills their minds with desires to know the Lord better.

Make this Eastertime a stepping stone to a new enthusiasm for the Risen Christ. Cry out frequently: "The Lord is risen, Alleluia." I have found this helpful to sing out throughout the day. Also: "The Lord is Great. God is Awesome. Three Cheers for the Lord. Hurrah for the Lord." When our hearts beat with joy for the Risen Lord's presence among us, prayer comes easily to our lips. A Blessed Eastertime to all our readers!

1994 Pilgrimage To Jerusalem

February 7, 1994, Monday. On this sparkling day of warm sun and fresh breezes, I walk from my guest house, Notre Dame of Jerusalem, down the steep hill to the Damascus Gate, one of five gates in the Old City. For two Israeli shekels (66 U.S. cents), I take a jitney minivan to Emmaus, a seven-mile ride.

Emmaus, where the Risen Christ met the two troubled disciples on Resurrection morning, lies in the hill country to the north of Jerusalem. In this Arab community, a worn-out asphalt road, about the width of a car, serves as the one and only thoroughfare. How easy for me to picture the two grief-stricken followers being met by Christ, in disguise, on this road!

A Franciscan priest opens the door in the high wall, surrounding the Church of Emmaus, and greets me with an overflowing good spirit. Much like a 20th-century St. Francis, the poor man of Assisi, the priest has holes in the knees of his pants, a stocking cap on his head and an old coat. What a joyful heart he has as he seems to jump and skip about in our walk to the church!

In the cold church, which seats about 200 people, I offer Mass. The Gospel this day tells the story of the broken-hearted disciples being met by the Risen Lord. In the sanctuary above the altar, a sculpture shows Jesus seated at table with His two followers, one by the name, Cleophas. Of all the visions of Christ at Eastertime, this visit at Emmaus has always held first place in my heart, probably because so often I have felt discouragement and weariness of spirit. No one else is in the church.

After Mass—which I thoroughly enjoyed in a special way (maybe because I offered it for myself)—I spent an hour walking up and down in the chilly atmosphere of the church. In the silence, the Lord promised me the grace of a happy death and many other inspirations because of my pilgrimage to this holy place. "I will help you face the circumstances surrounding your death. Do not fear!"

. . . the priest has holes in the knees of his pants, a stocking cap on his head and an old coat.

A wild ride brought me back to Jerusalem. At times I thought this would be the "happy death" the Lord was talking about!

The thought came to me in days after this visit to Emmaus: "Why do so many of us feel unhappy and troubled?" Could this be you?

For some reason, my work in the marketplace has lost its sense of fulfillment. I pull myself out of bed, reluctant to face another day with my co-workers. Many friends have dropped out of my life in recent times. I know the fault is mine. My heart is heavy with a sadness that brings gloom and darkness to my home and family.

I can cure this malaise by bringing the Risen Lord with me to my work, to my friendships, to my home life. The disciples despaired when Christ was absent. How different life became when He stood with them!

"Lord, come with me!"

My Favorite Hymn

The hymn I treasure most is *Come, Holy Ghost:* "Come, Holy Ghost, Creator blest, and in our hearts take up Thy rest. Come with Thy grace and heavenly aid to fill the hearts which Thou hast made, to fill the hearts which Thou hast made."

On weekday mornings, when I celebrate Mass in neighboring parishes, I always begin with *Come, Holy Ghost.* Certainly hearts in this context does not refer to our physical hearts, but rather to our inner spirit, our soul, the dwelling place of the Holy Spirit.

Often, each day, I whisper a prayer: "Create in me, O Lord, a clean heart"—words taken from Psalms. Let us treasure our hearts! My heart is the seat of all my emotions: joy, peace, love, kindness, forgiveness. From my heart proceeds my ideals, my hopes, my ambitions. How priceless a possession I have in my heart where the Holy Spirit lives in glory and everlasting Beauty!

If I saw the Holy Spirit in my heart, I would die of intoxicating joy. This Beauty outshines all beauty of Nature as the sun outshines the light of a candle. In life, we face an array of powerful enemies—the world, the flesh, and the devil—determined to deface our hearts and rob them of their holiness. Television, the great communicator, pours a torrent of pagan ideas and ungodly messages into our front rooms all hours of the day.

In the Gospels, we hear of even Jesus being tested by the devil. Jesus had prayed for 40 days in the desert just before these temptations, so He had quick answers to the wiles of the devil. How encouraged we should be that Our Savior showed us the way to deal with temptations. Our weapons of defense lie in prayer, the Eucharist, and the help of the Blessed Mother.

A few years ago, at a Priests' Conference, a nationally known priest speaker made these amazing remarks to 600 priests: "We priests would do much better ministry for the Lord if we worked four days a week, spent another two days in study and prayer, and then took one day off . . ."

My heart is the seat of all my emotions, of joy, peace, love, kindness, forgiveness.

Prayer was to hold the top place in the priests' daily life. Whatever my vocation in life, prayer and vigilance will enable me to keep a clean heart in all my temptations!

If I keep my heart pure and unspotted from the world, then my thoughts, my ideals for life, and my holy ambitions will flow from an unpolluted source. Peace, only the kind of peace that Jesus can give, will possess my being. Use my favorite prayer often . . . "Create in me, O Lord, a clean heart!"

I Was Hungry, Thirsty, A Stranger, Sick, In Prison

I have visited the top of Mt. Thabor a number of times. According to Scripture scholars, Mt. Thabor in Galilee, in the northern part of the Holy Land, served as the setting for the Transfiguration of Christ. As the three Apostles—Peter, James and John—saw the Glory of Christ, they cried out, "How good it is for us to be here." How we wish we had such an experience!

On a Monday morning in March, I was on Mt. Thabor and saw Christ transfigured. As I sat in my car, parked on the street at 22nd and Indiana Avenue, near the downtown district in Chicago, I saw a street man walking up and down the sidewalk, next to my parking spot. In past months, I had seen him in this same routine. While waiting for my appointment with our *Airport Chapel Bulletin* printer, I had time to observe the middle-aged man.

On this cold, windy morning, he wore a dirty jacket and pants, with a disheveled beard and no hat. In his hand a wine bottle top appeared above a brown paper bag. Just 20 feet from me, he sat down on an old blanket in an unused doorway. This was his home! From a white, plastic carry-out box—something he had picked up from a street garbage can—he put a few fries to his lips and some other leftovers. He appeared to treat these as delicacies. Soon he curled up in his doorway to sleep, drawing the poor blanket over himself.

Then the words of St. Matthew, in Chapter 25, came to my mind. "I was hungry, thirsty, sick, in prison, a stranger, naked, and you served my needs," Jesus said.

How shocking! Jesus identified Himself with all these unfortunates! At this point, I saw a blaze of Glory and Light come forth from the little man cuddled in the doorway. "Lord, it is good for me to be here," I cried out. I believed the words of St. Matthew!

Just 20 feet from me,
he sat down
on an old blanket in an
unused doorway.
This was his home!

What did I do? I prayed fervently for the homeless man that a better life would come for him. A gift of money would have sent him to the nearest liquor store. Some may say this man chose this life for himself. But Christ never made judgments on the poor He met. Even with miracles, He tried to better their lot!

As we meet the derelicts of life, the poor, may we see the Glory of Christ shining from their faces! Pray for them at least! The Midway Airport Chapel gives 10% of its income to two charities in our community!

A Stranger On The Road

January 9, 1994, Friday, Jerusalem, 2:00 am. In the cold night air, Tom Mescall, 49, a lawyer from Albuquerque, New Mexico, waits outside the Notre Dame of Jerusalem Hotel for a taxi to the Ben Gurion Airport in Tel Aviv. For business reasons, Tom, a member of our pilgrimage group, is leaving for the USA several days before schedule. Out of the darkness, two men approach to share the taxi with him to the airport. From the golden chains on their chests, my friend concludes they are Bishops.

At the start of the hour ride to Ben Gurion, one bishop introduces himself as Bishop Francis George of Yakima, Washington. The other Bishop heads a diocese in South America. Despite the early hour, Tom and Bishop George engage in a lively conversation about living a Christian life in a violent world. Why have people lost a sense of personal responsibility ? At this time, the Tanya Harding story and her poor treatment of her professional skating competitor is holding the headlines. Both lament the decline of moral values in the USA.

My friend plies Bishop George with many questions about the future of the Church in the Third Millennium.

The Prelate responds frankly about his own opinions. At times he punctuates his remarks with lighthearted laughter. At the airport they go their separate ways with warm good-byes and promises to pray for each other. Often, in the past few years, Tom has spoken to me of this meeting with the pleasant stranger, Bishop Francis George.

April 8, 1997, Tuesday. At last, through TV coverage, I meet Archbishop Francis George, newly appointed to Chicago. Now I understand why he had so much influence on Tom Mescall. I see his warm smile, relaxed demeanor, self-confidence, and his ability to laugh at himself. His whole manner cries out friendliness and good will. I say to myself, "This man is enjoying life."

Out of the darkness, two men approach to share the taxi with him to the airport.

This encounter of Tom with Bishop George that night in 1994 reminds me of the meeting of the Risen Christ with the two despairing disciples on the road to Emmaus. With utmost kindness, Jesus explains why it was necessary for their Master to suffer and die. His gentleness captures their hearts and forces them to cry out, "Stay with us. It is towards evening."

In past years, I have often celebrated Mass in the Church at Emmaus. In my times of darkness, I meditate on this appearance and found a new sense of peace and hope for the future. The Lord is walking with me, I say to myself.

On the road of life, the Lord joins us in our low spirits, in times of discouragement, on beds of suffering, in places of violence. He will support and heal our troubled hearts! The new Archbishop of Chicago gives us a good image of the Risen Christ, One willing to reach out to everyone crossing His path.

St. Peter's Cathedral, Rome

The Crucifix In The Church Of Saints Gervais And Protase

Across the Seine River from Notre Dame Cathedral in Paris stands the ancient Church of Sts. Gervais and Protase, martyrs in the early days of Christianity. Inside this Gothic-style church, I always find an atmosphere of semi-darkness where huge, round pillars hold up the high ceilings. What attracts me especially to this church is the larger-than-life crucifix hanging from the side wall.

Each time I stand before this cross with Christ hanging on it, I always have one thought: "I will do my best to avoid sin!" Christ agonizes in a way that I have never seen in any other crucifix. His head turned sideways and upwards tells of the hideous pain exploding in His brain. From the strain of the agony gripping His legs and arms, the muscles have twisted themselves into grotesque rolls of flesh, all cramped and bulging.

As I stand there, I can almost hear the shrieking of the human part of Christ, filled with shock and violent trauma, crying out for relief. Through the years, this crucifix on the side wall of the old church, in the half-light of winter afternoons, has reminded me that Our

Savior did not buy our salvation cheaply. Sin, large or small, is not something to toy with carelessly!

Many years ago—some 38 or so—a friend gave me a crucifix he had carved from rough, tough wood. As I kiss the Face of Christ—which I do every morning at Mass—I am in danger of picking up slivers. My friend did not make the Body of Christ smooth and antiseptic as most crucifixes are fashioned. In the Face of the Suffering Christ, the sculptor made deep lines to portray the excruciating suffering of the agonized Lord. As I hold this precious gift to my lips and sense as never before the physical and psychological pain Jesus endured, I am forced to cry out, "Lord, do not let me betray You today!" In the Holy Week ahead, let us hold on to our crucifixes deep within our hearts!

His head turned sideways and upwards tells of the hideous pain exploding in His brain.

Come Alive

Several years ago, in the Holy Land, I was walking across the top of the Mount of Olives on my way to Bethany where Martha, Mary, and Lazarus lived in the time of Jesus. Behind me, to the west, lay the Holy City, Jerusalem, all aglow in the early morning sunlight. Rain had fallen that night, making the downward path a slippery one to walk on.

Suddenly, my feet flew from under me, and I landed flat on my back on the wet, clay road. My pants had clay clinging all over them. As I sat there, catching my breath, I imagined a voice saying to me, "Arise, George, from your bed of clay! Come to life! Stand up and be renewed! Throw off your ways of death!"

Just ahead of me, a few hundred yards, at the foot of the hill, stood the tomb of Lazarus at Bethany, where Jesus had called out to the dead man, "Come forth, Lazarus!" With clay covering his funeral wrappings—the same kind I had on my pants—Lazarus did as Jesus commanded him and took his place again in the home of his sisters.

"What a coincidence!" I thought. I wouldn't be able to remove the clay from my pants for the rest of my stay in Jerusalem. In the days that followed, the clay reminded me of my mortality and the short time left to me in this life. "Thank you, Lord, for this spill on the Mount of Olives. O blessed fall! I must make something of my life before I return to the clay of the grave."

In the past, on airplane trips, I would bring a heavy bag and a light carry-on valise. This big bag caused me much exhaustion and frustration all through these trips. Recently, I simplified my life by bringing one pair of pants, one pair of shoes and a few washable items—with the result that I can lift my bigger bag with two fingers. My travels took on a new excitement and enjoyment. Perhaps, we are toting too much luggage as we move through these days of life: too much anger, resentment, finger-pointing, anxieties, despair, and fears. These make up the wrappings of death, acting as barriers between us and God. In the clothing of life, love, kindness and unselfishness—fill our days with light. How about simplifying this journey through life? "Come alive," Jesus says.

. . . catching my breath, I imagined a voice saying to me, "Arise, George. . ."

My brother complains when I play golf with him. "You are always trying something new—in your stance, grip, or backswing!" He's right, because I am forever trying to improve my golf score. (I am the Champ of the Retired Priests of Chicago—285 in number—for the last five consecutive years, so there is a method to my madness.) Why not do the same with this game of life? Try many different things to make a better score! Why keep making the same mistakes?

He Entered Into The Spirit Of Christ

Seven years ago, around Palm Sunday time, a friend of mine, a resident of Albuquerque, New Mexico, enjoyed an unusual experience. A few days before Palm Sunday, a group of people in his local parish asked him to play the part of Christ in the Living Stations of the Cross. The original person chosen had taken sick. Tom, my friend's name, hesitated because of the tightness of his schedule as a busy lawyer and probate judge.

This role, as the Christ, would involve memorizing many words that the Lord spoke in the last hours of His Life. Tom's common sense said, "No"; but his heart said "Yes." As Tom told me himself, this role playing of Christ, on that past Palm Sunday, affected his life greatly in an uplifting way. In a spirit of faith, he put his heart and soul into the words Jesus used and into the actions the Savior went through on His way to Calvary. For that time, Tom looked out on life through the eyes of Christ.

Because of his exhausting enactment of the Lord's Life, a burning desire sprang up in his spirit to learn more about Jesus of Nazareth. Since that Palm Sunday in 1988, my friend has come with me seven times to the Holy City of Jerusalem. God has rewarded him with gifts of peace and joy for taking on that role of the Christ those years ago. Now in his late 40s, Tom still finds himself trying to think and act like the Savior in his days in the law courts of Albuquerque, New Mexico.

I propose this goal to our readers. During these next five weeks of Eastertime, try, as St. Paul said, to "Put on the mind of Christ." As my friend Tom did, look out on life through the eyes of the Risen Lord. During this time, after the Resurrection, the Risen Savior went about as a Messenger of Peace. How often He greeted His friends with the blessing: "Peace be with you!" We can imitate Him by being people of peace these days of Eastertime.

For that time, Tom looked out on life through the eyes of Christ.

Yes, Our Lord showed Himself a Peacemaker, an Encourager to down-hearted people, a Forgiving Person to His Apostles, a Joy-filled Friend to all whom He met, a Bringer of Hope to His fearful followers. We wish to follow in His footsteps this Eastertime by being the kind of Person Jesus was! Say often, "What would the Risen Lord do if He were in my shoes?"

Acting out the Life of Christ could work wonders in our spirits by bringing a glorious peace, a wish to know the Lord better and an effectiveness in helping others never before thought possible.

The Feast Of The Divine Mercy

What a fantastic story we have in the life of Helena Kowalska. Born in 1905 in a small town in Poland, the third of ten children, Helena entered the religious Order of Our Lady of Mercy at age twenty, after being turned down by a number of other Orders. For her religious title, Helena was named Sister Faustina of the Blessed Sacrament. Because of her poor health, her superiors gave her menial jobs about the convent—doorkeeper, cooking, gardening. Here in Krakow, Poland, this humble, sickly woman delighted to live in this atmosphere of prayer and peace, little realizing what the future held for her: a surprise from God!

In 1931, the Lord began to appear to Sister Faustina, telling her that He wished her to spread the message of His Divine Mercy to the world. These frequent visits continued until her death in 1938 from tuberculosis. Fortunately, Sister Faustina kept a diary of the Lord's messages, a journal that would come to 600 pages. In April, 1993, Pope John Paul II beatified Sister Faustina, thus giving the complete approval of the Church to all these happenings in her short life.

I used to associate just one meaning to the word

mercy, namely *forgiveness*. However, in the last two years, mercy has come to embrace all words connected with love in action, such as healing, curing, raising others from their miseries, encouraging others in their depressions, concern for others. This realization has uplifted my life tremendously! When I call Jesus the Lord of Mercy, I just don't think of forgiveness, but also of all those loving actions I just mentioned. As He often told Sister Faustina, He wants to be this Loving Person to each one of us. "Tell My people to come to Me with complete trust."

... this humble, sickly woman delighted to live in this atmosphere of prayer and peace ...

Sister Faustina proposed a simple plan for us to follow for giving respect and devotion to Our Lord of Divine Mercy—and that is the ABC schema. This has helped me to keep this wonderful story uppermost in my thoughts.

(A) Ask for Mercy. Go frequently to the Lord (perhaps the reader has an Image of Jesus as He appeared to Sister) and beg for an outpouring of His loving actions into our lives. Desire greatly!

(B) Be Merciful. Bring a blazing spirit of love into our thoughts, words and actions. Determine to look upon all whom we meet as friends of the Lord of Divine Mercy. Treat all with respect and love.

(C) Completely Trust. The more hope we have that

the Lord will give us the gifts we ask for, the more surely will they come to us. If I bring a small water glass of trust to the Fountain of Mercy, that amount only will I receive! If I bring a big bucket of trust, imagine how much more I will obtain!

If Only I Came To Know Christ Sooner

This experience has happened to me frequently. As I turn on the radio, I hear the last bars of a favorite piece of music, maybe Beethoven's Fifth Symphony. A sadness fills my heart. How I would have enjoyed hearing this masterpiece from the beginning! I turned on the radio too late. Has the reader gone through this kind of sadness?

We can transfer this experience to our life story. What if we should see the Grandeur and the Glory of the Person of Christ in the last weeks or days of life? Here I am on my deathbed, when suddenly, by inspiration or a heavenly vision, I glimpse the Attractiveness and the Greatness of Jesus of Nazareth. I cry out, "I wish I had seen the Splendor of the Lord sooner when I was young and healthy. What a difference this would have made in my life!" A terrible sadness will chill my heart.

In March, 1995, we buried a young woman of 35 years of age. She left behind a grieving husband and two little boys, ages five and three. From childhood this person had always been a faith-filled Catholic, but about two years before her death a sudden inspiration took hold of her thoughts and mind. Somehow the Person of Christ captured her heart and desires, pushing her to spread the Kingdom of God in her community. Her enthusiasm encouraged many other young women her age to join with her in working for holiness in their parish.

In her last months of life, as she bore patiently many sufferings, she told me of the new excitement and delight that came into her life on sensing the Beauty of the young Preacher from Nazareth. After her death, I began to look into my life, with the determination to latch on to a new Vision of the Lord of Life and Death. I don't want any deathbed sayings, "If only I had..."

I don't want any deathbed sayings, "If only I had..."

Perhaps our days follow one after another in gloomy fashion, a dreary procession of uninspired happenings. How quickly this would change if we captured this Vision of the Messiah, Jesus of Nazareth! A new excitement would enter our lives and fill our days with an unexplainable happiness, no matter what our crosses might be. We would live above our own immediate needs and cares to think of how to spread the Kingdom of God as this woman did.

On this Palm Sunday, witness the enthusiastic shouts of the followers of the Lord as He makes His way into Jerusalem on the back of a donkey. For a brief moment, these delirious people saw what a noble and humble person Jesus was, as they hailed Him their King. Sad to say, this fervor lasted only a short time. During Holy Week, be present in a loving way at the ceremonies honoring our King, Jesus of Nazareth.

The Touch Of The Master's Hand

From my favorite paperback book of poetry, *The Treasury Of Religious Verse,* I found much food for thought in a short poem entitled, *The Touch Of The Master's Hand.* An auction was taking place, and the auctioneer hardly thought it worthwhile to waste time on an old, dusty violin.

"What am I bidden, good folks?" he cried. "Who will start bidding for me? A dollar, a dollar." Then: "Two, only two! Who will make it three?"

As he sang out these words, an elderly man came forward from the back of the room and picked up the bow. Then, wiping the dust from the violin and tightening the strings, he played sweet, enchanting music. After the music stopped, the auctioner spoke quietly, "A thousand dollars! Two thousand! Who will make it three thousand? Once, twice, going, gone for three thousand!"

"What made the difference?" the people asked in amazement.

The reply came quickly, "The touch of the master's hand."

At this time of life, many may find their lives out of

tune. The sweet music of youth has given way to the sour, discordant noise of pessimism, unloving ways of living, spitefulness, unhappiness at the success of others, to refusals to change suicidal ways of coping with life.

Perhaps many see themselves in that dusty, old violin, their lives unappreciated by others about them, little value placed on their presence. Into such lives as these, Jesus, the Master of Love and Hope, can step, tighten up a few strings, and play glorious music. Didn't this Jesus say, "I am the Bread of Life. No one who comes to Me shall ever be hungry, no one who believes in Me shall thirst again." (John 6:35)

Yes, the Touch of the Master's Hand can turn our lives around in a short time to true loving attitudes towards others, to a spirit of hope for the future, to a quick growth in self-discipline. How much do we believe in the words of the Master Musician, Jesus, the Prophet, just mentioned above? In the days ahead, I'm going to Christ in prayer and tell Him of all the gifts of the spirit I am hungering and thirsting for: peace, joy-filled days, a greater love of the Mass and prayer, holiness of life, love for all crossing my path, and a host of other riches like patience, courage in facing life, and the acceptance of pain.

At this time of life, many may find their lives out of tune.

The key word is believe. Believe in the words of the Lord. Remind Him of His promises in John 6:35. Too often, we try to accomplish these works of the spirit with our own human powers. Doomed to failure, we spin our wheels in frustration. I'm turning to the Lord so that He can play glorious music through my poor, little life!

The Precious Gift Of Mary To Us

In my daydreams, while wide awake, I rejoice in the possibility that I could spend some part of my last days living in the shadows of Notre Dame Cathedral in Paris.

Over the years, many such dreams have come true, such as missionary work with the Eskimos in Alaska and opening a chapel of worship in Midway Airport—other dreams, too. To daydream pays dividends.

In my many visits to Paris, I always made Notre Dame Cathedral the center of my day. This magnificent monument of stone built in honor of Mary, the Mother of Christ, stands as a reminder of the faith of the French people of a 1000 years ago.

Notre Dame Cathedral in Paris, France.

Constructed over a period of 100 years, with four generations of architects, the mighty Cathedral cries out to all entering its doors: "Believe in Mary, the Mother of God! Treasure her Love!"

In my daily wanderings to the Cathedral, I made my way to the foot of the famous statue of Our Lady, situated to the right of the main altar. Always surrounded by flowers and burning candles, Our Lady of Notre Dame stands on a pedestal, looking with gentle concern on all praying before her. I would like to spend some quality time in this place in the last part of my life!

The more I love Mary, the more will be my love for her Son.

As I sat there in these daily visits, the surroundings of the Cathedral gave fuel to my spirit of prayer . . . the huge pillars, the exquisite stained glass windows, the semi-darkness, the fervor of people of all nations kneeling before Mary, and sometimes the beauty of music played on the Cathedral's organ.

Many times my heart felt heavy within me as I thought of my future work in the priesthood. Why did the Lord choose me, with the few gifts He gave me, to preach a message many people refuse to hear? Mary had a Son, a Priest. She would understand the murmurings of my heart. I found immense peace in this place at Mary's feet, far away from home with no schedule to follow and with no earthly concerns on my mind. What a special person to share life with!

A Sister of Mercy, Sister Mary Ambrose Griffin RSM, deceased at the age of 98, had her lifelong motto printed on her Funeral Mass program: "To Jesus Through Mary." She died in a spirit of holiness—no danger of loving Mary too much! The more I love Mary, the more will be my love for her Son.

I encourage our readers to find such a place of prayer at the feet of Our Lady, maybe a statue at home or a painting on the wall. Homesick for heaven? Struggling with life's many challenges? Ready to stop a noble work in building up a holy family? Sit at Mary's feet; pour out your story!

Beautiful statuary grace the walls of Notre Dame Cathedral.

To Jesus Through Mary

Several years ago, my older brother suffered an illness that left him without speech. One morning, to the amazement of his family, he began singing a hymn our mother sang to him as an infant in arms:

> *Mother dear, O pray for me when far from Heaven and thee. I wander in a fragile bark on life's tempestuous seas.*

The words came from his lips with clarity. After this, he fell back into speechlessness.The memory of the peace he enjoyed in our mother's arms broke the bonds of his tongue. He sang in desperation in his need for help.

Our mother—Mary her name, now deceased thirty years—was following her son with love and concern in his time of darkness and challenge. She was lifting up the spirit of my brother with words sung almost 80 years ago. A mother's love wants the best for her child.

We are all children of Mary, our heavenly mother. On the cross at Calvary Jesus gave us Mary, His own mother, when He spoke to the Apostle John and Mary: "Woman, behold your son. John, behold your mother." As in the story at the beginning, our Mother Mary follows us through life with a love beyond all understanding.

Mary wishes to lead us to her Son, Jesus, because He is the source of all happiness. At Bethlehem she brought Him into the world and presented the Holy Infant to the three Magi. In our own day, she desires us to come into a close friendship with this Saviour Child. Through the ages, the cry of the Church has been "To Jesus through Mary (Ad Jesum per Mariam)."

The memory of the peace he enjoyed in our mother's arms broke the bonds of his tongue.

In speaking to the world on December 8, 1978, Pope John Paul II stated, "Mary is called to lead all people to the Redeemer . . . Her vocation is to bring all people closer to her Son."

I Am The Bread Come Down From Heaven

On Saturday, August 2, 1997, the Vice President of the USA, Albert Gore, and his wife, Mrs. Tipper Gore, came through Chicago Midway Airport on a short visit to our city. Of course, this caused a flurry of excitement, as people tripped and fell over themselves in efforts to see the famous couple.

A few hours later, that same day, another great person visited Midway Airport, though without the fanfare and outcry of the Vice President's arrival. In Gate B-12, I pronounced the words of Consecration: "This is My Body . . . This is the Cup of My Blood . . ." at our 4:00 pm weekend Mass—and the Lord of Heaven and Earth, Jesus of Nazareth, came down on our humble altar. The One sent by the Father rested on the white cloth under the appearances of bread and wine. With no agents to protect Him, the Lord of the Gospels came among us to be our food and drink, unconcerned about His own safety.

This Coming didn't create a big stir in our Midway Airport, the busiest middle-sized one in the world. A few, faithful followers of the Lord, gathered in a makeshift place of worship at Gate B-12, bowed their heads in worship. For thousands of others at this crossroad of America, it was just another dull day of waiting for their planes to take off. Mass was well publicized over the PA system.

Recently I read some shocking news in the *Catholic Extension* magazine. The writer stated that a 1994 *New York Times/CBS* poll disclosed that 70% of Catholics under the age of 45 did not believe in the Real Presence of Christ in the Holy Eucharist. Presumably, according to their way of thinking, the water and wine, even after Consecration by the priest at Mass, are just symbols of His Presence. Our belief in the Real Presence of the Lord in the Eucharist makes up a foundation stone of our Catholic Faith. What a tragedy if denied!

With no agents to protect Him, the Lord of the Gospels came among us to be our food and drink, . . .

In the neighborhood where I presently live, an Adoration Chapel, located in a former convent, opened its doors almost four years ago. On its altar, a monstrance holds the Blessed Sacrament, exposed for all visitors from 9:00 am until 9:00 pm. In my visits to this chapel, I have seen comparatively few people under the age of 45; so, perhaps, the above poll holds some truth. Either that or, a crisis of faith has come to young Catholics.

Who am I to pass judgement on anyone? There are enough things in my own life to be sad about! But should not all of us examine our lives to see how strong are our beliefs in the Presence of Jesus of Nazareth in the Blessed Sacrament? After writing these words, I am going to start a personal crusade in my own faith life to light a fire of love and devotion for the dear Christ of the Blessed Sacrament, so unheralded, so little sought after!

After years of doctoring, a woman touched the cloak of Jesus. She received healing. I, too, will touch His cloak for healing.

Serve God While There Is Yet Time

This past month of July, 1996, while recuperating at home from a hospital stay, I received a phone call from the West Coast, from a former student of 50 years ago. Jim, now 61 years old and a resident of California these past 25 years, thanked me warmly for the help I gave him in Maryville Academy.

Fifty years ago, Maryville Academy, located near Des Plaines, Illinois, had 850 resident boys and girls between the ages of 5 and 17. Because of conditions at home, these normal and healthy youngsters lived the year round on the Maryville campus. Among many things, Jim mentioned a homily I had given to the children one Sunday morning at Mass 50 years ago—the shortest homily (called "sermons" in those days) of my priesthood.

Always convinced that the children (and older people) remembered and appreciated short "speeches" (as the boys and girls called them), I turned to them this one Sunday morning at sermon time and for 20 seconds looked out at the 300 children gathered in the school chapel. With their attention focused on me, I solemnly spoke these words, "Serve God while there is yet time."

After another pause of 20 seconds, I went back to the altar to continue Mass.

Over the next several weeks, the "speech" by "Fadder" (as they called us priests) served as a red-hot topic of talk on the campus. In our phone dialogue, Jim stated that the words of the homily have stayed with him all through the past 50 years, a saving message for him in his efforts to love God.

"Alleluia!" I said to myself. I, too, have never forgotten my shortest homily. Serve God while there is yet time! Now, 50 years later, there are many fewer days left me than on the morning I spoke it, as a young priest of 27 years of age. Twenty of my priest classmates have left on the Glory Road for Heaven. Thirteen of us still remain, blessed with chances each day to work for God's glory and praise. The Gospel says, "Work while there is still light. . . . No one can work in darkness."

Are there some fences to be mended before Judgement Day, long-standing disagreements in the family circle?

I encourage our readers to put the words of my "speech" in some visible place in their homes, like on a refrigerator or on the mirror in the bathroom. Keep the realization of the swift passing of time always before us! Are there some fences to be mended before Judgement Day, long-standing disagreements in the family circle?

Am I putting off the confession of my sins until some future time?

At my front door, a little plaque tells me as I leave, "Each day is a precious gift from God." Take advantage of the time we have to worship God in His Holy Sanctuaries, to love Him by keeping His Commandments, to share ourselves with all His creatures in a caring way!

Starvation Comes Under Many Guises

Our hearts go out to the starving children of the world! Through the miracle of TV, these boys and girls come into our front rooms and fix their sorrow-filled eyes on us, the viewers. We can count the ribs in their weakened bodies and can only commiserate the bloated condition of their stomachs, a sure sign of starvation in progress. Without proper nourishment, the human body grows desperately weak and open to all kinds of diseases.

Many commentators write about the scourge of starvation of the soul taking place in the USA. Once St. Paul wrote, "We live in evil times." He could write the same words about our present days in the 20th century.

Look about us! Our prisons are bulging with criminals, with not enough jails to go around. Among the young, many find a way out of life through suicide because they do not believe in a God of Hope. Mental hospitals take up more than half of the beds available with the disease of depression setting new records—abortions, drug addictions, serious juvenile crimes, low attendance at churches of all faiths, domestic battering, the scourge of AIDS. God rests on the shelf!

To face these desperate conditions, all of us need to test ourselves daily for signs of spiritual starvation. If we fail to feed our soul, it, too, like the body, will fall into weaknesses with sad results. An alarm should go off in our mind, if we notice some of the following things happening:

- I am continually depressed about life.
- My complaints fill the air with no one able to please me.
- Anger at everyone, a chip always on my shoulder.
- I have stopped praying.
- The Eucharist has lost its meaning for me.
- I go to church with a heavy heart, counting the minutes until the service will end.
- How boring life is!

Of course, the chief source of nourishment for the soul comes in the Holy Eucharist, the Person of Christ. All the qualities that the Lord possessed in the Gospel stories come with Him into the Eucharist and into our inner life—His kindness, gentleness, courage, His loving attitude towards all. As He enters our temple, He leaves these riches on our pulsating hearts that we may absorb them into the bloodstream of our being. For fifteen minutes after the reception of Holy Communion, the elements of His Body and Blood remain with us. In these moments of divine intimacy, what inspired sharing about life and its weary happenings could take place between the Lord of Love and ourselves! Such prayer brings health to the soul.

Unfortunately, many consider the Eucharist as a reward for good living and thus absent themselves from the table of the Lord for long periods of time. Jesus comes not as a reward but, rather, as nourishment for the health of the soul. If free from serious sin, we can hurry to accept this food from heaven wherein we will escape from starvation of the spirit and its disastrous consequences!

. . . all of us need to test ourselves daily for signs of spiritual starvation.

"O Miracle of Miracles, the Eucharist of the Lord!"

Keep Your Eyes Fixed On Jesus

Someone may ask me, "How did you persevere in your 51 years plus in the priesthood? You have lived through many stages of life from teen years in the seminary up to senior citizen status at present. We can understand how youthful enthusiasm and dreams of saving the world could move you through the early years in the priesthood; however, for the long haul, when the bitter reality of life has gripped your heart, something—a powerful motivating force—had to come into play. You have gone through two different Churches, the pre-Vatican II one and the post-Vatican II one. The big exodus of priests in the 60s must have disturbed your mind about continuing in the ministry. What kept you going?"

I would answer that I agree with all the above statements. My response may appear too simple. I left the seminary at Ordination time with the words of St. Paul emblazoned on my heart: "Keep your eyes fixed on Jesus." (Hebrews 12:2) See how the Lord persevered in His work as Messiah, even though He saw the sufferings and disappointments He must undergo!

St. Paul lived out his own advice. "In shipwrecks twice, scourged with whips many times, betrayed by brethren often, chased out of towns. I have been hungry and thirsty . . ." (2 Corinthians 11:25) Paul persevered in his vocation. All through my priesthood, I have tried to keep my eyes fixed on Jesus. If I hadn't, I wouldn't be here today as a priest. In all the perils and struggles of the Priesthood, He stood as a role model for me, as my Saviour and Messiah.

At different times, things like vanity, ambition, and the attractiveness of women would fight to take on a greater appeal than the Master. A bell would sound in my heart. I knew that the time had come to go back to the drawing board—to my original plan of action—to keep my eyes fixed on Jesus.

. . . the attractiveness of women would fight to take on a greater appeal than the Master.

How did I do this? I built up His appeal and beauty in my heart by sharing my life with Christ more deeply in prayer, by some forms of penance, and by reading His life in the New Testament. My many pilgrimages to the Holy Land helped me to appreciate the preciousness of my ministry as a priest. I could not give up my calling as His minister for some earthly gain. To these efforts, the Lord always responded with love and peace. I would be the last one to say that these pulls and tugs of life in the world were easy to deal with. The human heart was made to love and be loved. I can easily understand why many priests left to get married.

Our readers can learn from my life story! In any vocation we find dangers and challenges. In married life commitments are made, to be kept all through life. Keep your eyes fixed on Jesus. We don't want to trade the friendship of Christ for a passing whim.

Altar of Crucifixion in the Church of the Holy Sepulcher, Jerusalem. Father McKenna offered Mass frequently on this altar and the altar of Sorrowful Mother.

Resurrection Story

Over the years of my life, one stage play, a musical, *The Man of La Mancha,* has inspired me to a deeper appreciation of our Lord's love for us. Its setting lies in the Middle Ages. In the story, a gallant knight in his travels meets a woman of low reputation, one rejected and scorned by her townsfolk. No one is encouraging her to rise up from her sad state of life. The poet knight, however, sees virtue and goodness in her true nature.

From the first meeting, he affirms the woman with unconditional love. This love says, "You are good! God loves you. You are precious to Him. He doesn't care about your past. Believe in His undying love for you." At first, she rebels against his efforts, but gradually she begins to take his words to heart and throws off her old way of living. No one had ever spoken to her in this way. A new life begins for the once despairing woman.

In time, the Christian knight gives her a name, Dulcinea—a name meaning "sweetness"—and he keeps reminding her of her beauty and loveliness. On his deathbed, calling her to his side, he reminds her again of her name, Dulcinea, and sings the famous song *The*

Impossible Dream. "To fight the unbeatable foe, to reach for the unreachable star, to bear with unbearable sorrow, to dream the impossible dream... This is my quest!" This was his final encouragement to her to help her persevere in goodness!

In my thinking, *The Man of La Mancha* stands as a parable of the love the Risen Christ, the Lord of Divine Mercy, has for all. Dulcinea comes across as a Resurrection person, rising from death to a new life of goodness. In disbelief, many cannot accept the unconditional love Christ has for us. They ask, "You mean the Lord has the same love for all, no matter what our past track record has been?" Yes, He has the same respect for saints and sinners, and all in between. All share equally in His love. Believe wholeheartedly! Enter into the spirit of Resurrection time! The Risen Jesus can bring to life habits of goodness we thought long dead.

Objections fill the air: "I haven't prayed in years." "My love for God has died out, only ashes remain." "My heart lies like a stone within me, with love for no one there." "I can't see God's presence in this violent world." "Despair has captured my heart." "After all these years of unfaithfulness, I can't see the Lord loving me!"

Believe it or not, the Lord's love for us has never stopped, but He needs our cooperation to make this love effective in our lives. In the story above, Dulcinea changed when she opened her heart to the message of unconditional love coming from God. Go and do likewise! Dream *The Impossible Dream*!

The Holy Spirit Moves In Our Family Life

On Saturday, August 16, 1997, I was just finishing our Midway Airport 4:00 pm Mass in Gate B-12 with the words "The Mass is ended, go in peace and joy and serve the Lord and each other with much love." At that moment, a great jet plane, a DC-9, rolled by the distant window with only one word on it . . . SPIRIT . . . with the letters the height and the length of the fuselage of the plane. In the congregation facing me, not one of the 80 people could see this apparition except me.

I had never seen such a plane—with this word, Spirit, on it—in all my nine years at Midway Airport. For me the message came loud and clear that the Spirit of God was moving through our little family of worshippers gathered in Gate B-12, even though no one was seeing this holy happening.

In our modern age family life is taking a beating as never before. Too many distractions send family members in all directions with the resulting loosening of family ties. In a belief that the Holy Spirit is a close member of our family circle, we shall have courage to say what Joshua (1200 BC), the successor of Moses, proclaimed to the Israelites on their entrance to the Promised Land: "As for me and my household, we will serve the Lord."

Believe that the Holy Spirit, the Person of Love and Holiness, is deeply interested in the success of our family life, even though we do not see this presence in our homes. Every day, we can pour out our hopes and desires to the Spirit for our family's progress in closeness to God. For all of us, the picture may appear dark and hopeless at times—but persevere! Keep repeating Joshua's words—"As for me and my household . . ."

. . . not one of the 80 people could see this apparition except me.

At the Last Supper, Jesus took a towel and washed the dirty feet of His Apostles, a work the lowest servant usually carried out. At the end, Jesus said, "As I have done for you, so also, you do for each other." Be a positive member of the family circle; encourage others in the pursuit of their goals; if asked, advise them; do favors for others in the household. The Holy Spirit, a dear Friend to all, will inspire us.

In other words, fill your home with a spirit of love, no matter how little the effort is appreciated. Actions speak louder than words! My brother does my laundry for me every week without pay and my sister lights a big candle for me every Saturday morning in church. These things mean much to me.

At the evening meal, we have an excellent chance to celebrate family life. If possible, set a peaceful atmosphere with candlelight, no bright overhead lights. No serious conversation allowed—let everyone tell of the funny happenings in their day, exulting in each other's presence.

Bread, The Staff Of Life

Some years ago, on an oppressively hot summer morning, I boarded a train in Rome, Italy, bound for the far northern City of Turin to visit the Shrine of St. John Bosco (1815-1888). Little did I know that the train would stop at every little station on the way. With no air-conditioning or dining car, I was asking for trouble when I took this train for the 12-hour ride to Turin.

On the seat opposite me sat an elderly American couple, Mr. and Mrs. Henry Moore from Kansas City, two gracious, kind and cultured people, as I was to find out in the hours ahead. Knowing that I was a priest, Mr. Moore told me of his work as a sculptor in fashioning the huge front doors of the recently completed San Francisco Cathedral. In a photo he showed me, the doors, reaching some 30-feet high, portrayed many Old Testament scenes in bronze. This work on the San Francisco Cathedral, a world famous church, identified Mr. Moore as a world-class sculptor.

As the hours rolled by, I grew conscious of my hunger and thirst. Finally, we came to Carrara, the place where the famous Italian marble is quarried, the stopping-off place of the Moores. After warm goodbyes, I felt the train moving out of the deserted station. Suddenly Mr. Moore came hurrying across the platform with a fresh loaf of bread and a bottle of red wine and thrust them through the open window into my hands. This highly-placed man had noticed my predicament and took time to satisfy the hunger and thirst of a lone stranger in a foreign country. I have never forgotten the Moores and their exquisite thoughtfulness!

In the Scriptures we read of the considerate actions of another highly-placed Person feeding scores of hungry people in a deserted place. Jesus, the Prophet from Nazareth, saw the plight of the crowds listening to His Words and provided a good supply of bread for their bodies.

This highly-placed man had noticed my predicament . . .

Not only did Jesus satisfy the hunger of many that day, but at the Last Supper, on the night before He died, He made certain that His followers, in the centuries ahead, would never die of spiritual hunger. At that Supper, in a most serious way, Jesus said over bread and wine, "This Is My Body . . . This Is My Blood . . . Do This In Memory Of Me . . ."

Because of His amazing Love for all His people, Our Messiah thought up an almost unbelievable way of Himself being the Food and Drink for His needy followers. Much as Mr. Moore came rushing to me in that train station so many years ago with delicious bread and drink, so, too, does Jesus approach us with His Holy Bread and Precious Drink. In our weakness and failing strength, we eagerly reach out to take these Gifts from our Gracious Provider.

We Discover God In Prayer

In years gone by, I found my best consolation in prayer, a conversation with God. Without watering down the truth, in the priesthood I've sometimes found preaching and teaching to be difficult and unrewarding. Full-time teaching duties took up the first 25 years of my priesthood. I certainly tried hard enough! To keep myself in the priestly ministry, I had to turn to prayer as never before. Since I didn't find satisfaction and consolation in the work at hand, I might have given up the priesthood for a more fulfilling position in life.

So, each day, as a priest, prayer became the mainstay of my carrying out my duties in the church. In morning prayer, I threw my arms around the knees of the Lord of the Gospels with a plea for His help and encouragement through the day. In the midst of darkness, poor work results and occasional conflicts, friendship with Jesus of Nazareth through prayer took on a new preciousness and delight. Maybe failures need not be so evil!

If someone asked me where did I find my most happiness and inspiration these past years as a priest, I would answer this way. Especially in the quiet, dark chapels and churches of Paris, I experienced an unbelievable uplift of spirit. Some writers call France un-Christian and irreligious, but nowhere did I find such splendid places of worship as in Paris.

God appears so real in the Gothic-styled churches with their soaring ceilings. With no schedule to follow—alone—I would go in from the noise of the traffic in Paris to share my thoughts with God, the Father, the Son and the Holy Spirit. Time went by quickly. My failures and conflicts with others lost their depressing effect as I thought of the Beauty of God and His Saints.

Time went by quickly. My failures and conflicts with others lost their depressing effect...

In Jerusalem and its neighborhoods, I discovered new depths of riches in prayer. In these fairly dark—and usually cold—grottoes and chapels far from home, the attractiveness and the wisdom of sharing life with Christ oftentimes overwhelmed me. These discoveries bring me back time and time again to the Holy City of Jerusalem. I have stayed in the priesthood only because prayer—conversing with God—has shown me that failures and successes are quite the same with the Lord. What Jesus, the young Rabbi from Nazareth, wants is a heart dedicated to Him and His Father's Glory. Through daily prayer, we can offer ourselves to this end.

Over the years, I have always tried each day to spend an hour of prayer before Christ in the Blessed Eucharist. From the words above, may readers gain some ideas for their own personal growth in a life of prayer—such prayer is a totally joyful and uplifting experience.

Joy Can Make Life Heavenly

The word *joy* ranks as the most precious word in our English vocabulary, outside of our Names for God. The one who possesses joy has a treasure beyond all others. To all—yes, to everyone—God offers this gift of the heart, a happiness of the spirit, a long lasting light-heartedness.

During Advent time, we hear St. Paul reminding us often, "Rejoice always in the Lord!" Not just on some days, but always. Not only in sunny days of success and good health, but also in the dark hours of life. The joyful person has peace in his heart, a freedom from fear and anxiety, an optimistic attitude towards the future, a spirit of goodwill towards all.

What price must we pay to have joy in our spirits? Christ has to have first place in our hearts! There, He rules supreme with no other false idols of sin present. Yes, joy demands a high cost, that we love this Lord and treasure His presence above all things.

A while ago, I drove to downtown Chicago on the windiest day in the last 80 years, with gusts up to 60 miles an hour. Of course, I didn't know when I started out that I would experience such a traumatic day. I parked on South State Street. With all my strength I held on to light poles as I made my way down Dearborn Street. At Congress Parkway, a six-lane expressway, I hugged a traffic pole at midpoint for a long time. With no buildings to block the wind from the east, the gusts tugged at every inch of my body. I thought the end had come.

At home that night, I found my arms black and blue from bruises, from the intensity of my holds on the life-saving light poles. "What can I learn from this stressful experience?" I asked myself. A light went on in my mind. I will hold on to the Lord, my God, with the same determination that I used on those poles. Jesus told His disciples, "Love Me with your whole heart, with your whole soul, with your whole mind, and with all your strength . . ."

With no buildings to block the wind from the east, the gusts tugged at every inch of my body.

My spirit of joy depends on this Lord! I will not let Him go from my heart, no matter how strong the evil winds in life are tugging at every fiber of my being to betray Him. Then my heart will have this gift of joy beyond all measure.

Why not set your sights on this quality of joy which brings a taste of heaven into our lives and brings laughter and happy sounds to our lips? J-O-Y = Jesus Only You.

Advent, My Favorite Season

Some years ago, on a cold afternoon in January in Paris, France, I came upon a church of breathtaking beauty, St. Nicholas in the Fields. All bundled up in my parka, I planned to spend an hour in this Gothic masterpiece—despite its freezing temperatures—praying about my priesthood. However, during that hour, I was breathing in the icy air with no scarf over my mouth. I paid dearly for this mistake. For the next week I was sick in bed, with much discomfort.

In our present day, we live in an atmosphere of violence, indifference to God and immorality. Eighty percent of the movies made this year of 1995 had an R-rating. In our cocoon we may think that we are all bundled up against this presence of evil. So we move along blissfully, without taking precautions, not realizing the dangerous conditions we live in. How easy for us to succumb to the sickness of personal sin, despair or some form of personal violence!

Advent, a favorite penance season of mine, has arrived with the beginning of another Church Year. These three weeks before Christmas sound a wake-up call to each one of us. "Hey, stop!" it shouts. "Look into the condition of your soul, into your friendship with God. The Prince of Peace is coming."

I enjoy walking through my neighborhood at twilight, seeing the lights in the windows, a symbol of hope for the future. On the radio the carols tell of a Child of Promise, Who comes to bring us peace. If we enter into this Holy Season with prayer and some mortification, we will find strength to fight off the evil all about us. We will capture that peace that we so yearn for!

In past days, remarkably, almost unbelievable things have taken place. In Bosnia, Northern Ireland and in the Mideast (Israel and the Palestinians), all at once, a promise of peace has come. A year ago, no one would have predicted this sudden turn of events! Hope of a normal life for the people of these troubled countries now looks like a possibility. God has heard our cries for peace in the world.

God has heard our cries for peace in the world.

At this Advent time, 1995, wonderful happenings, too, can come to pass in our souls, in our home life—events that we would never have believed possible. Maybe a peace of heart that we haven't experienced in years will be ours. Someone in our home circle will throw off an addiction to drugs, alcohol or depression of mind—all because we lived through this Advent time with much faith in God, Who calls us to holiness of life.

Be aware of the troublesome days we live in. No human powers will save us from the corruption surrounding us. Pray; do some penance; cry out to God, as I do every day, "Jesus, help us."

A House Restored

During this past summer of 1994, in neighboring Evergreen Park, I frequently drove past an attractive brick residence, with its windows all boarded up because of a flash fire that gutted its interior. In early November, various tradesmen, under the direction of a contractor, parked their trucks outside this sad-looking home and began the work of renewing the interior. Carpenters, plumbers, electricians, interior decorators and painters are now pitching in to make this home a delightful place to live in. At Christmastime, a fire will be burning in the fireplace. A Christmas tree with its colored lights will tell of the happy spirit within.

At this Advent time, I want to look at my spirit as a house with interior fittings and facilities. I will use the pronoun "I," not only to refer to myself, but also to all the readers of this article. Like those tradesmen, I can pull up in front of my house. Perhaps many features inside lack attractiveness and make life unpleasant and unfullfilled. I will pay close attention to these eyesores and replace the rotting wood of despair with fresh lumber of hope, anger with meekness. Perhaps a new furnace will give warmth to my heart!

I notice the house of my spirit has a run-down appearance, because my zest for living has drained away in recent times. I can't get enthused about anything, especially about God and His Kingdom on earth. The covers on the windows indicate my lifestyle of cutting myself off from friends and neighbors. Just leave me alone in my poor spirits! Everyone wants to argue with me. I don't know why. Maybe it's because I start the argument first.

I need God to help me in this renewal of the home of my spirit! God (the Father, the Son and the Holy Spirit) will give me power and direction if I go to Him in prayer.

The covers on the windows indicate my lifestyle of cutting myself off from friends and neighbors.

Allow me to show a good practical way to pray for Advent. In September, 1994, at our International Airport Chaplains Annual Meeting in London, the priest speaker encouraged the 80 people present to use this age-old method. In the morning, choose some line or phrase from one of the 150 Psalms.

Today, as I wrote this bulletin, I chose these words from Psalm 25: "Lord, teach me your paths." Through the day, I have been saying that line to myself and adding some personal thoughts. "Lord, I want to walk in your footsteps, to be a person like You, in Your gentleness and kindly ways." The Psalms have hundreds of such simple, inspiring phrases.

The speaker in London gave this assurance. "From the beginning of the day, you will have a theme which will encourage you to say your chosen phrase frequently as you go through your day's work." I personally have enjoyed my prayers today.

Look closely into the house of the spirit. Decide what is bringing a chill and darkness to this real home within me.

The Dark Nights Of The Soul

Like all normal human beings my age, I have lived through many dark periods in my life. For me, during these times, the world was about to come to an end. I lost interest in living. Joy left my spirit.

One might ask, "What brought about these dark feelings?" I could mention many ordinary experiences, such as sicknesses, failures and lack of success in my work, misunderstandings with co-workers and parishioners, overwork, concern for family members and friends—all contributed to gloomy times that tried my soul. When I was ordained a priest, I thought everything would be smooth sailing. How naive I was, what little understanding I had of life.

In these dark days, I would hang on for dear life to the hem of the robe of the Master in hope that better times would come. After a lapse of time, without fail, my spirits would come back to an even keel. How glad I was that I didn't throw in the white towel in the terrible darkness of the preceeding days. As the years went on, my philosophy came to be, "Never give up. Never!"

Especially in past Advent times, if I were going through a troublesome stage of weariness and apathy, I would hear Isaiah speaking out about the coming of the Messiah. The Savior will come to lift me up from the depths of darkness, to support me with His love and strength. With my last bit of energy, I would keep repeating, "Come, Lord Jesus. Come, Lord Jesus!"

All human beings go through these trying times. No one can escape these life experiences. Perhaps some people reading these lines find themselves in a room of darkness and depression. The walls are moving in, closer and closer. "All is over. I will give up. My heart is breaking." A voice keeps repeating these words in their spirits.

"All is over. I will give up. My heart is breaking."

Maybe we have lost our jobs. Sickness won't leave us. Bills are piling up at a staggering rate. Family life has turned into a battlefield. A long-time friendship has come to an end, or we may grieve for family members and friends deceased. In our present Advent Season, the words of the Prophet Isaiah, can touch our hearts with hope for good times to come:

> *Here is your God. He comes to save you. Say to those whose hearts are frightened, "Be strong, fear not." Strengthen the hands that are feeble. Make firm the knees that are weak.*

The Messiah comes to be reborn in our hearts if we put out a welcome sign for Him. As the Light of the

World, He will dispel the dark spirits of gloom and despair within us. The more we hope, the more fruitful will this Advent time be! Expect great things to happen! "Come, Lord Jesus."

Suppertime, A Blessed Event

Many years ago—1959—I remember sitting down to a meal in a little hotel next to the stormy Atlantic Ocean in Enniscrone, in western Ireland. A blustery, raw day raged outside, but, inside, I sat next to a glowing hot stove in the company of friends with a mouth-watering dinner set before us. Comfortable in each other's company, we dined, while listening to the two young people present reciting poems and singing ballads, a memory never to leave my mind. All those adult friends have died since that time.

In the family evening meal, we can find precious moments for growth in love for each other and tranquillity of spirit. Even if we live alone, as I do, we can make supper a time for personal uplift and joy. With darkness wrapping the world outside in mysterious shadows, a family gathers together for the sacred ritual of the evening meal in the warmth and coziness of its little castle.

What matters is not so much what is on the menu—although that helps greatly—but, rather, what is in the minds and hearts of those coming to the table. Approach the family table as one would the altar in the church! In His Providence, God calls us together to renew our bodily strength and to grow in our appreciation of each other.

As all come together—with faces washed, hands clean and hearts delighting in each other's company—a peaceful stillness creeps into the assembly. Our meal prayers remind us of God's daily care for us. Am I painting too rosy a picture of family life? I hope not!

Eat slowly! Look around the table to discover new greatness in the lives of each other. These meals will provide rich memories of consolation in the years to come. Treasure them now! In the dining room, a semi-darkness can add a mystical, magical setting to the family circle. Candles, possibly a soft light in the corner and quiet music contribute to the overall mystery of what is taking place. Too much overhead light destroys the illusion of coziness and peace. All stay to the end of the meal—most important!

Even if we live alone, as I do, we can make supper a time for personal uplift and joy.

Only lighthearted conversation takes place at these moments of the evening gathering, no matter what troubles happened during the day. Laughter, the telling of jokes, the recounting of the happy moments of the day can make the suppertime a delight and a joy! When close to death and looking back over life's happenings,

I am certain that memories of meals shared with family and friends will fill my mind most of all.

Who Will Open My Ears?

A few years ago, doctors in a Chicago hospital placed a 5-year-old boy in a tent-like structure filled with pure oxygen. His little body could not fight off infections from germs and viruses. In this unnatural, little world, he found himself cut off from the hugs and kisses of his parents and from all contact with the outside world. One day he died unexpectedly, to the great grief of all.

As time went on, the story took on a new significance for me. At certain times, I could see myself living in such a self-made structure, in the rarified atmosphere of my own selfishness. With my mind filled with my own problems, I would cut myself off from all those about me, even those crying out for help. This isolation added misery to my life. I might as well have been deaf and dumb. Surely, at times, such a condition must affect the life of the reader!

Recently a major airline at Midway Airport gave seminars to its thousands of employees on the importance of giving cheerful and effective help to their passengers. One main theme came across in these meetings: "Listen to the voice of the person. Perhaps you will detect weariness, hostility, anger or fear. Respond to that emotion in the voice! Soothe the anger! Ease the fear! Promise personal help to the weary! Give everyone equal treatment—the poor, the rich, the well-placed, the illiterate!"

How well we could use that theme of the above seminars as we strive to listen to the voices about us, crying for help at this Christmastime 1997! First, be willing to listen! "Lord, unplug our ears! Loosen our tongues." We need not be experts to give assistance to those in need. Speak simply from the great wisdom in our hearts, a wisdom residing there from our experience in living. Respond compassionately to the emotions in the voice of the person in need.

Speak simply from the great wisdom in our hearts.

Be A One-Person Revolution For Love And Peace

Last year, 1995, close to Christmastime, I offered a Funeral Mass for an elderly friend. His painful sickness of five years certainly brought him a quick entry to Heaven. With only sons and no daughters, with his wife in a nursing home, several daughters-in-law stepped in to help him through those five years. Call them surrogate daughters! In his last hours, my friend suddenly sat up in bed and cried out words, difficult to understand. Did he want ice cream, good health or a reprieve from pain? No! With much effort, he got out his message, "I want a hug!" His daughters-in-law finished off their work of years of unselfish love for him with warm hugs.

Can we ever emphasize enough the power of a hug, an expression of love and concern? No! In any language, the three most powerful words for good are "I love you!" At home and in the family circle, the best gifts we can give at Christmastime come in expressions of love and gentleness. Material gifts soon disappear or are forgotten, but loving words and actions linger in minds for a lifetime. Determine to be a one-person revolutionary for love and peace in your home!

Recently, at a morning parish Mass with school children in attendance, I told the boys and girls, "See the Lord as an infant in arms. Really, our Saviour has no age. Carry Him about in your arms as you do your little brothers and sisters. Talk to Him about your secret fears and worries. Especially hug Him tightly and tell the Holy Child your love." Many weeks later, the school secretary told me how much she enjoyed this idea and how she had done this in her own prayer life with much profit to her happiness.

Material gifts soon disappear or are forgotten, but loving words and actions linger in minds for a lifetime.

At this Christmastime, why can't we do the same? Are not we adults children at heart? Our Messiah, as an Infant, is no different than our Saviour on the Cross. Find much joy in holding the Christ Child close in your arms, so innocent and helpless. In this cold world, He wants our hugs and tenderness! How quickly the Child of Mary would win over our hearts and help us proclaim a reign of love and peace in our homes!

In this coming Holy Season of Christmas, we can be channels of God's peace in our family circle by expressing our feelings with words like: "Have I told you today how much I love you? I love you more than I can say. Thanks for all the good things you do for us."

As For Me And My Family

In a phone conversation a few days ago, a lawyer friend of mine in Albuquerque, New Mexico, told me of a recent experience of his. Just east of his home city stands the imposing mountain range Sangre de Cristo (Blood of Christ), its loftiest peak topping off at 14,000 feet. A client of my friend lives in a huge mansion, 7000 square feet, at the base of these mountains. On a recent visit to this estate, my friend Tom saw a verse from Holy Scripture on a foot-square bronze plaque, embedded in concrete, in the front lawn. "As for me and my family, we will serve the Lord." (Joshua 24:15)

Joshua, the successor of Moses, spoke these words in a farewell speech to his people, the Israelites. Under his leadership, his people had won the Promised Land for themselves after fierce wars. But now Joshua feared that false gods, so prevalent in the countryside, would win over the hearts of his people. The aging leader had seen his people fall into idolatry many times in the past. After his death, pagan gods replaced the True God.

Evidently, the family living in the great house in Albuquerque had decided this quotation from the Book of Joshua fit its spirit just right. "As for me and my family, we will serve the Lord."

At this Advent time, what a challenging and courageous cry we could make to the world around us if only we might unfurl a banner, with these words of Joshua enscribed on it, across the front of our home, pointing out to all passersby our willingness to choose the Lord and His ideals above all other things in life.

Yes, we do well to adorn our homes with colored lights, to symbolize our hopes of peace for Christmas soon to come. However, we may not be backing up these decorations with a firm decision to choose Christ as our Leader and Saviour. With the words of Joshua consciously before us, we might gather our family together and tell them the story of the family in Albuquerque. This takes courage, a willingness to face charges of being too religious. "As for me and my family, we will serve the Lord."

This takes courage, a willingness to face charges of being too religious.

Look, then, into your home and family life to discover if any happenings or attitudes compromise the words of our battle cry, found in the words of Joshua. Will the Christ Child, Whom we proclaim to serve, find in our house matters embarrassing to His Holy Presence, an attitude of reluctance to give Him public worship or a careless view of some of His Commandments?

If possible, without destroying the family circle, bring up the story of my friend and point out its wisdom and power for good! "As for me and my family, we will serve the Lord." What a fantastic Christmas your family might have!

Beware Of Thieves

This past month, in mid-November, a friend of mine came to Chicago from out of town for his father's funeral. While Tom, my friend, was swimming in a local pool, a thief stole his pager wristwatch—something he treasured greatly. Nine years ago, he bought it for $450, and since then this little marvel of technology had served him faithfully. "Why didn't I use more caution in safeguarding this special possession?" Tom is saying to himself. Thousands of messages came to him and Motorola no longer produces this pager.

In every corner of life, thieves and demons lurk, not only to steal our earthly possessions but also our riches of spirit. In Midway Airport, undercover police constantly scan the crowds for the professional pickpockets. At this Advent time, we might look into our inner life to see if wicked angels have stolen treasures from our hearts without our knowing it.

Just as car thieves focus on certain makes of autos, so the demons from Hell make every effort to steal away our spirit of prayer. Here is the deceitful trickery they use to rob us of this most precious gift: In dark moments of our lives, they plant the seeds of doubt about the value of prayer. "Why pray? God doesn't hear you. You haven't received any answer to your prayer! It's a waste of time." In weakness, we may listen and stop talking to God.

A reader might be saying, "I used to raise my mind and heart to God at different times during the day. I delighted in sharing my life with my Heavenly Father in my happy moments as well as in the dark hours. Through these communications, I felt a closeness to Him. In turn, He spoke to me of many things and guided me in ways of goodness. Now, I hardly think of God during the day—in fact, not at all! Seemingly, He has removed Himself from my life. No messages come to uplift my life, to bring light in times of darkness. I feel depressed and unhappy about life."

The demons have robbed this person of the spirit of prayer.

The demons have robbed this person of the spirit of prayer. If this is our case, we can bring back this gift into our hearts by simply spilling out our thoughts to the Lord, to the Father, to the Holy Spirit in an outburst of faith. "O God, I believe, I believe!"

The Holy Spirit, True Friend

As I set out on my pilgrimage to Jerusalem this January of 1994, I am deeply conscious of the work of the Holy Spirit within me. In the sacred places around the Holy City I can relax and be quiet, with no telephones ringing or appointments to think about.

I will invite the Holy Spirit to enter my heart as a Spirit of Love, as a flaming fire to burn away all the waste accumulated there over the past months. In this time of peace and quiet, the Spirit will in some way speak to me—a whispering voice, a prodding motion, a hungering for something better, a wishing for higher things.

Once I read through a Christmas gift book and, almost at the last page, I discovered a colorful ribbon book marker. It had escaped my notice. Within each one of us are many undiscovered qualities. We are strangers to ourselves! A consciousness of the Holy Spirit, the Amazing Guest Who lives within us, can lift up our lives to new heights of glory.

I never sit down to write without first putting "VSS" at the top of the sheet—"Veni, Sancte Spiritus" or "Come, Holy Spirit." By this act of faith, my mind is open to the inspirations of the Spirit. As iron is permeated with flame in a fiercely burning fire, so did Jesus allow Himself to be totally open to the Holy Spirit in His days on earth.

As I walk the Via Dolorosa, or sit in the Garden of Gethsemane, I will, as never before, be alert to the presence of the Spirit of God, conscious of my Friend's Powers to transform my life and bring out the best in me. This Person wishes to bring enthusiasm for living into my life, a sense of wonder at each day's happenings.

Within each one of us are many undiscovered qualities.

Even at my advanced age, I believe there lies a world within me yet to be discovered. A human being is always on the way, in a process of fashioning himself. A new age could be just around the corner. At this Holy Season of Lent, all of us can find an ideal time to cry out to the Holy Spirit, "Come, Holy Spirit, and in our hearts take up Thy rest."

Cynicism, pessimism and despair defeated the work of Jesus, and even to this day it continues to defeat Him. Surrender yourself to the Spirit this Lent of 1994! The fruits of the Spirit are joy, peace, patience, gentleness, and kindness.

Do You Love Jesus?

On January 28, 1995, at the Annual Prayer Breakfast in Washington, D.C., a former Senator approached the Speaker's table in his wheelchair. In the hearing of the distinguished assembly of Christian Congressional leaders, including President Bill Clinton, he whispered these few words into the microphone. "There are only two questions in life. Do you love Jesus? Does this make a difference in your life?"

With death close to him from a brain tumor, this former Senator, once a dynamic orator on the floor of Congress, reduced all issues in life to these two questions. We ask ourselves these questions. Certainly, we love Jesus, we quickly assert, but have we decided how this makes life different for ourselves?

Certainly, we love Jesus, we quickly assert, but have we decided how this makes life different for ourselves?

As followers of the loving Christ, are we showing His love to the world by our lifestyle? Our Savior wishes us to be witnesses to His love. As people see us living our daily lives, are we giving them a picture of the Christ of the Gospels? By our peace-loving ways, our willingness to help in time of need, we can give our neighbors an example of care and concern. Yes, these people will say, this is the way that Christ would live, we have a better understanding.

Cenacle Chapel in Jerusalem. The site of the Last Supper is just fifty yards from here.

The Adventure Of Seeking The Lord

Some years ago, on a cold, gray March morning in Paris, I boarded the TVG, the fastest train in France, with a speed of 135 mph, to visit the world renowned monastery of Taize. I was curious to meet the founder of this holy place of prayer, Brother Roger Schulze, a man of my age in his seventies, a close friend of the last four Popes. The two-hour train trip went by quickly.

A bus ride of forty-five minutes brought me from the railroad station of Macon-Loche to this utterly unpretentious village of Taize—made up of one street, ten homes and the monastery buildings. To this difficult-to-reach place come young people from all over Europe all through the year, to seek peace and an inspiring vision of the Lord.

At noon a church bell sounded the assembly for prayer in the Prayer Building with Brother Roger and his forty white-robed monks. Almost a thousand people filled the place—cozily warm, dimly lighted with flickering candles—an ideal setting for prayer. The music, low-keyed, sounding almost like a continuous murmur, brought a pleasing sense of joy and peace.

At much personal sacrifice—with only simple food

on the menu and Spartan living conditions (sometimes in tents)—these youthful adventurers of the spirit come to renew their hopes and visions of life. During one Holy Week, ten thousand young people had made Taize their home, camping out and sharing their dreams with each other in prayer groups.

Almost a thousand people filled the place—cozily warm, dimly lighted with flickering candles—

As Lent comes upon us, we feel conscious of a yearning in our hearts for a clearer vision of Jesus of Nazareth. Like the young pilgrims of Taize, we realize that nothing material or earthly can satisfy the hunger of the spirit, only the experiencing of the closeness of the Lord. I went away from Taize convinced that the adventure of prayer exceeds all other human strivings.

What brings these youngsters, with their backpacks, long distances to hear this man of God talk about Jesus of Nazareth? Read these lines from Brother Roger's book *The Adventure of Seeking the Lord*:

> *When your hopes are disappointed, would you let yourself be submerged in discouragement and doubt? The Christ is in you. Your trials, the thorns within you, are consecrated by His fire, and even the stones in your heart, through Christ, can become glowing coals in the darkness.*

Would that we had the verve of the young pilgrims to seek out Christ in these precious days of Lent, 1994! I will always treasure the experience of seeing these youngsters at prayer, with their desire to know the Lord of Light!

Enthusiasm Is Everything

Over the years I have met many interesting people in my work as chaplain at Midway Airport. After sharing thoughts about life with these men and women, I often found myself looking into my own hopes for the future.

One Sunday—February 11, 1996—a strong, young man about 45 years old, the Reverend Mark Sawyer, minister of a small church in Bemidji, Minnesota, dropped into the chapel to say hello. His eyes sparkled as he congratulated me on the presence of the chapel in the airport. One could see that he was a man taken up with the cause of the Lord. He went on to say, "I'm on my way to the Promise Keepers' Meeting of the Clergy in Atlanta, Georgia, this coming week."

Forty thousand ministers and priests were coming together in Atlanta, Georgia, to prepare themselves for the eight Promise Keepers' Meetings scheduled in the months ahead across the USA, with an average attendance of 60,000. The meeting in Chicago's Soldiers Field, June, 1996, expects 65,000. Not a new religion or political party—the singing of hymns, the fellowship and the dynamic preaching have done wonders in the lives of men.

The Promise Keepers, started four years ago, brings together men of all faiths and races for the sake of committing themselves to Ten Promises. One promise asks the men to give witness to Jesus Christ by their holiness of life and public testimony. Another promise tells men to love their wives and build up their families in Christ! A third promise reminds men to be pure in all ways.

"Mark," I said, "are you excited about this meeting?"

He responded, "Just feel the goose pimples on my arm. We are going to immerse ourselves in the thrilling story of Jesus of Nazareth. I need these days to remind myself of the possibility for change in my life."

He responded, "Just feel the goose pimples on my arm. . . ."

Nothing successful or rewarding takes place without passion, that is, an enthusiastic, absorbing interest in what one is doing. Watch someone at his or her job! If this person throws all into the work at hand, wonderful things happen.

We enter Lent this week, an enthralling 40 days of excitement, as we pursue a deeper closeness and friendship with Jesus of Nazareth. Do we have goose pimples on our arms, brought on by the excitement of the blood racing through our veins? Do we feel ourselves stirring with strong feelings, terribly enthused about the possibilities of coming to know Jesus, the Messiah, better than ever before?

Pray these days before Lent on what we wish to accomplish! Are there ways of acting or attitudes of mind that hold me back from being a close follower of Christ, the Lord? Take part in Lent with enthusiasm! Pray, do some penance, read!

The Mysterious Garden

Prayer is the key that opens the door into a Mysterious Garden. When I used to hear the words "Mysterious Garden" in my childhood days, chills would run up and down my spine. Wonderful and surprising things could happen in this Garden of Mystery.

I open the gate in the high wall that surrounds this Garden. I walk in and start down a pathway of stones. Suddenly, in front of me, I see Jesus of Nazareth sitting on a bench, the Friend of sinners, the poor and the helpless. His friendly welcome, His kindness make me feel at ease.

How surprising! I don't have to join a line of people reaching to the horizon to wait for a few words of welcome from the Exalted One. On a visit to Rome, a friend of mine shook hands with Pope John Paul II. He looked upon this as a high point of his life. How this experience fades into insignificance beside my meeting in the Mysterious Garden with this Jesus of Nazareth, the Lord of the Universe, the Master of Life and Death, the King of Kings.

Encouraged by the complete attention He gives me, I begin to share with Him many ideas and hopes close to my heart. Now and then He rises from the bench and picks rich, juicy-looking fruits from nearby trees. He places them in my pockets and hands. At times the Gentle Christ reaches down to pluck various colored flowers from the ground and shiny, bright stones from the pathway. This is His way of saying, "You are important to Me. I care for you."

What a privilege! I am never alone.

Soon I rise from the bench, with pockets and hands filled with these gifts from the Master. A new peace has come into my heart. His Friendship lifts me up. How considerate of this Great Person of the Gospels to give me all this time for conversation on matters close to my heart.

What a privilege! I am never alone. This Mysterious

Pope John Paul in the Vatican City.

Garden is always there waiting for me to enter and sit with the Master, the All-patient, the All-loving Friend. My faith will guide me there often.

In all the twists and turns of life, sickness, crushing failures, loveless treatment from others close to us, personal falls from human weaknesses, Christ followers find themselves severely tested. We cannot give up in despair. Prayer will help us to face life with courage.

“Go In
Peace
To Serve
The Lord
And Each
Other
With Much
Love!”

—Father George McKenna

About the Author

Father McKenna, the youngest son of Irish immigrants, spent the first 25 years of his priesthood as a teacher—first at Maryville Academy, then at Quigley Seminary. At Quigley, he was the spiritual director, guiding young high school seminarians in learning ways of righteousness and prayer. During the second half of his career, Father served as pastor and associate pastor at several parishes on the southwest side of Chicago. He also spent some time as a missionary in the Fairbanks, Alaska diocese.

As Father neared retirement, he took on the challenge of establishing a chapel at Chicago's Midway Airport, which was experiencing a rebirth. Although *technically retired,* Father has now moved into his third career, ministering to air travelers and airport employees.

A lifelong resident of Chicago, Illinois, Father McKenna has been a world traveler, seeking inspiration across the globe. He has made twenty pilgrimages to Jerusalem. Father's favorite places to visit and write about are the Holy Land and Paris, France.

For fun, Father enjoys playing a good game of golf. He is the six-time Senior Golf Champion of the Retired Priests of Chicago Association.

After 54 years in the priesthood, Father McKenna continues to fulfill his life's mission of encouraging people everywhere to love God and others.